Golden Linings II

More Tiny Tales about Pets, for Pets

ISBN: 978-1-943201-27-3

Library of Congress Control Number: 2019944278

Graphic Design by Darin M. Peters.

First published by AM Ink Publishing: July 15, 2019.

AM Ink Publishing
Southwick, MA 01077
www.aminkpublishing.com

AM Ink Publishing and its logos are trademarked by AM Ink Publishing.

The publisher is not responsible for websites (or their content) not owned by the publisher.

Published in Southwick, MA, the United States of America.

Golden Linings II

More Tiny Tales about Pets, for Pets

Edited by
Carol M. Ford

Graphic Design by
Darin M. Peters

I AM ink PUBLISHING

Our Mission

To help animals in need.
Author proceeds from sales of *Golden Linings II* are donated
to animal rescue organizations and shelters.

Official Endorsement

We gratefully acknowledge the following for officially endorsing *Golden Linings II*.

Introduction

The year 2018 was one of great difficulty for me. In early 2018, my father was diagnosed with a rare form of cancer—a Grade IV, terminal glioblastoma of the spinal cord. My dad had already been through and survived a lot in his life: high blood pressure, liver failure, double heart bypass, liver transplant, infections from immunosuppression, prostate cancer, and bladder cancer. And now, *this*. Throughout 2018, he endured more tests, a biopsy of the tumor, emergency surgery, and finally, radiation, followed by the wicked side effects that go with it: Now, he is experiencing paralysis caused by both the radiation treatments and the tumor. However, my dad is a fighter, and he is doing well. If his history can tell us anything, he will beat this like the champ that he is!

Over the past year, we have been surrounded with love and support from our family and friends. We stay positive and take each day as it comes. But when I'm alone with my thoughts and worries at the end of the day, my pets—my golden retriever Copper and my cat Charley—are there to provide the soft, comforting therapy I need.

Every pet I've ever owned has been a therapy pet—from my childhood, when I had trouble in school; to my unhappy marriage and eventual divorce; to today, whether it's because of my dad, stressors from the work day, or when I am frightened of what the future may bring. My pets have always been there in my times of need, calming my worried soul with their gentle, quiet understanding. They've brought me great peace, joy, and happiness simply by being there.

Last year, I decided to pay that back—and forward—with *Golden Linings: Tiny Tales about Pets, for Pets*, donating 100% of my author proceeds to our official endorsers, S.N.O.R.T. Rescue and Voorhees Animal Orphanage, and other shelters and rescue organizations as needed. *Golden Linings* has been so successful that my publisher and I decided to publish a second volume—*Golden Linings II: More Tiny Tales about Pets, for Pets*. As with the first volume, all author proceeds will benefit animal shelters and rescue organizations.

My hope is to have *Golden Linings* continue to grow and expand. Through *Golden Linings*, we can help animals in need. And they, in turn, can continue to help us through with their soft, comforting touch.

To everyone who has purchased *Golden Linings,* thank you! You are making a difference!

Carol M. Ford
Editor, 'Golden Linings'

Special thanks to Michael Aloisi and AM Ink Publishing, and to graphic artist Darin Peters for helping me make this book a reality.

To all who contributed photographs and stories of your pets, thank you for participating. You have my deepest gratitude and respect.

To all of my friends, thank you for your friendship and support. Always know I'm glad you're in my life!

And finally, to my family—my parents Bob and Jan Ford, my sister and brother-in-law Barbara and Jeff Reim, and my nephews Ben Reim and Adam Reim—thank you for always being there for me. I love you all.

---

www.goldenlinings.com

Boomer

There's very little I'm sure of anymore, but I know this. I miss him. I am also sure that Boomer's previous owner needs his butt kicked for the abuse. But after being declawed, neutered, and dumped, he found his way to my house. Boomer didn't trust easily, but he *did* trust us. I guess you get the seal of approval when they crawl up in your lap and lay down.

He chose us – and *we* are the lucky ones.

Such a tiny squeak for such a big boy, especially when it was time for the Blue Plate Special. We loved you, Boomer, as much as you loved your cheese. Someone would be fixing a sandwich or some nachos, and there was a little bite of cheese... *Oh Boy!*

If there was one thing Boomer loved – other than your catnip pickle and pepper – it was the warmth of the sunshine. And yesterday... Not a cloud in the sky.

We didn't even know about the tumor until five days before Boomer left us. I only wish there was more we could have done. I only wish I had the words. I held his head as he took his last breath. I didn't feel qualified, but I wouldn't have been anywhere else. I went outside and cried like I haven't cried in years. Drove home and prayed like I haven't prayed in years. Boomer's soul, his dignity, such trust and love. This was rare.

Boomer, you held our hearts in your paws.

Rest easy Boomer, you Magnificent Beast. Rest In Peace.

Dan Conley

Gilda

It had been two weeks since our cat, Junior, my best buddy for fifteen years, had passed away from heart failure. As much as we tried to carry on, we grieved. Something was missing.

One day, I stopped by a local shelter. There were several kittens available, all of them adorable. But a little gray tabby with a sweet face sat on a play area in a corner. She and her brother had been abandoned on the shelter's doorstep on a frigid morning a few weeks before. Her brother had just found a home, and she was now alone. I walked over to say hello. She crawled into my arms. Each time I tried to let her go, back up into my arms she went. She looked at me with those sweet eyes. And she purred just as vibrantly as Junior had when I held him for the first time. I finally told the assistant, "We may as well do the paperwork. I've been chosen."

It has taken no time at all for Gilda to earn her way into our hearts. She's goofy in the way kittens will be, but she's also incredibly sweet, spending hours sleeping next to me in a variety of positions that defy logic. She's already learning how to be my editorial assistant, keeping me company as I spend hours working on research projects, occasionally pressing a paw on the keyboard to add important details or delete content she deems extraneous. And when Gilda isn't chasing her stepbrother around the house, she's marching around with her head up and her tail erect. My husband calls her "Little Miss Gilda, large and in charge." Which she is—not only in charge of our house, but also of our hearts.

Jodie Peeler

Read Junior's story on page 19.

Cedric

Cedric, an African Grey Parrot, had been part of our family about ten years when one late fall day, I decided to clean the garage. Since temps were mild, I brought Cedric out with me and set him on his stand-alone perch. Before long, my wife came out to the garage and tossed something into an empty trashcan. That sudden, loud noise was all it took. In an instant, Cedric,took flight and headed straight out the open garage door. We watched helplessly as Cedric soared past our neighbor's house, banking left and upward. He was gone.

I spent the next five-plus hours searching for him, knocking on doors and looking in backyards, calling his name, then pausing to listen for a response. Nothing. After posting "Wanted – Missing Bird" posters on every telephone pole within a mile radius, I reluctantly halted the search. I was sure Cedric wouldn't survive the night outside, and every time I looked over at his empty cage, my heart ached.

At eleven o'clock that evening, I decided to search one more time before going to bed. I hopped in the car and slowly cruised down our street shining a spotlight into the bare trees, and that's when I saw a blur that didn't look like it belonged. I called out, "Cedric?" That's when I heard a whistle and saw a brief flash of bright red tail feathers. I'd found him! He was eight feet up in a tree, probably standing on the same branch he'd landed on at the end of his maiden flight hours earlier. I climbed up high enough to grab that branch, and Cedric immediately scurried down my arm onto my shoulder and started making kissing noises as he buried his beak in my neck. Hearing my feathered friend say "I love Dad" again was the happiest ending possible.

Cliff Henderson

Dodger

The month of November 2017 was very sad. We lost our little Yorkie Rocky after eighteen years.

I cried a lot, and my husband finally said, "Let's go to the shelters and see what we can find." Well, we went to four shelters, and they didn't have any smaller dogs, but we decided to try one more. We went to Camden County Animal Shelter, and when we walked in, this little dog was looking around the corner of his cage. I told my husband, "There he is." We asked the shelter staff to bring him out, and he was scared. He hid under the table, but eventually, he came around.

The next day, we went and picked him up, and we named him Dodger. He is a mixed breed of Yorkie and Shih Tzu, and he was three years old. Dodger is very lovable but also very protective of us. He loves to play with his toys, especially when they squeak. He sits, lays down, speaks when asked, and he loves to bark at the mailman. We love Dodger very much, and he makes us laugh and smile.

Margaret Fox

Circuit

Circuit was left at a pet store. No one wanted Circuit, and he was there for eight months. They called him White Lightning because he tried to escape at every chance. We rescued him before they made him the "store dog," meaning he would live there at the store, with no family, forever.

Circuit is loyal and kind, and not at all aggressive. He's playful and dances on his back legs when he's excited. He loves his dog bed and a good game of toss. He never met a person or animal he didn't like. Neck rubs are his favorite, and even though he doesn't like baths, he loves when the groomer comes to groom him!

Nancy Merritt

Junior

One day in 2003, a student asked if I wanted to adopt a little stray tabby she was caring for. It didn't take much persuasion. Two days later, she came to my office and put the little one in my arms. From that first moment, he purred. Loudly. That purr would be a constant in our lives for the next decade and a half.

We called him Junior, but there was nothing junior about him. He grew into sixteen pounds of mischief and love. He accumulated several nicknames, but the one that stuck—born from the stripes he wore proudly—was Junior the Mighty Tiger. But for all his professed ferociousness, Junior was a gentle giant.

Midway through Junior's life, we took in a young cat. Junior became the wise mentor, teaching his student the art of the mooch. As Junior aged into a distinguished feline gentleman, he spent more time content just to be near us, lying across my lap as I worked. The understanding he and I had with one another was uncanny, as if we were made for each other. When I felt stressed, he knew just when to give me a little kiss between my eyes.

For years, Junior had a heart murmur, and eventually, that mighty heart started to give out. One day, in our fifteenth year together, came the battle he could not win. As I held him for the final time, he purred as loudly as he did the first time we met, and he purred until the end came. I am sad that he is gone, but I am grateful for the years we spent together and all the love we shared.

And somewhere in the wild, I know, there's been born a tiger cub with a purr unlike any other.

Jodie Peeler

Monkey

Monkey came into our lives only weeks after we had lost our kitty, Bella. We hadn't planned on rescuing another so soon after, but it turned out to be a wonderful happenstance. I had gone to our local animal shelter to assuage my grief. One little kitten came up to me, put a paw on my leg, and made a sweet mew sound. She curled up in my lap without any prompting from me. How could I say no?

She was six months old and every bit the rambunctious kitten one might think. Our other kitty, Noodle, a five-year-old, nineteen-pound big boy, was quickly put in his place when she came to live in our home.

Now, at a year-and-a-half, Monkey has become a saucy diva, walking on tables (even though we tell her 'no'), claiming all the toys for herself (she will share, once she gets tired of something), and making squeaky noises at the window to the birds on the birdfeeder outside.

She loves to cuddle, play, chase Noodle up and down the stairs (sometimes he will initiate the game), and "help" in the bathroom. Apparently, she has decided we need supervision in most everything else we do around the house.

We don't mind a bit.

Sue Rovens

Baxter

I love my cat, and he loves me,
I don't let him out to climb a tree.
I keep him safe inside my house,
And let him try to find a mouse.

He searches high and searchers low,
He follows me wherever I go.
Even when I go to bed,
He climbs up and curls around my head.

If he gets hungry during the night,
He wants me to turn on the light.
And get out of bed to get him food,
Even though I'm not in the mood.

Half asleep, I go to his dish,
To put in some delicious fish.
Then it's back to bed I go,
He knows that I do love him so.

Even if I didn't awake,
And put some food for him to take.
I know that in his heart I'll see,
That he loves me unconditionally.

Cathy Peters

Anna

Anna was, without a doubt, the smartest, coolest, most loving dog I've ever had in my life. She was a Cockapoo, mostly black, with beautiful brown eyes that seemed to see straight into your soul. Her tail, a barometer of her mood at any given moment, was almost always whipping back and forth in happiness and excitement.

In the 1980s, I opened a video store. Since Anna was a puppy and couldn't be left home alone, I built a special place for her underneath the counter near the cash register, and Anna came to work with me every day, six days a week. She eventually got to know my regular customers, and more than a few would bring treats for her when they rented or returned their videotapes.

Anna was friendly to everyone, but she seemed to develop s special bond with the gals who worked at the hair salon a few doors down in the same plaza. In the warmer months, I would prop open the front door, which Anna took as a signal that she could come and go as she pleased. And she did! When I'd get busy in the store and eventually realize she was gone, I never got nervous. I'd just walk down to the hair salon, open the door, and there she'd be, curled up and sleeping smack dab in the middle of their floor just like she owned that place. Other times, after she'd had her fill of noise from the blow dryers, she'd walk herself back and take her place at my feet. I can still see her now, trotting back in the front door with her tail casually wagging, looking at me with an expression that said, "Yeah? And??? I'm back, aren't I?"

God, I miss her.

Cliff Henderson

Molly

This is Molly, a barn cat we took in. Our friend Linda has a horse farm, and stray cats end up in her barns. Molly was born there—a litter of three kittens. Linda has a heart of gold, and she neuters the cats and feeds them. Finding them homes is another story. Molly has a loving home with us but her two siblings are still in the barn. And an eight-week-old male tabby showed up in the barn just the other day.

Molly is just learning to be sociable. She tends to stay in secluded and tight places, behind couches, and under chairs. She is playful with our Maltese, Circuit. Molly is just learning what toys are. She's not fond of being held, but she tolerates being pet for short periods. And Molly loves to look outside!

Ben Merritt

Read Circuit's story on page 17.

Smokey

Our living room has a glass door along the back. Since we live in the middle of a forest, we often see the creatures whose woods we live in: deer, squirrels, turkeys, rabbits, and so many others. One day, a scrawny yellow cat, only about a year or so old, jumped up on the porch and spent the afternoon snoozing. It was kind of cute. But the cat kept coming back about the same time each day. We took to calling him Transient Bonus Cat. Since I'm unable to let any of God's creatures go hungry, I began putting out a little food for him. He was a friendly little cat and enjoyed the company.

In time, Transient Bonus Cat would run to meet us at the side of the house when we brought his food. He didn't want us to leave him, either. One day, as I went back inside, I felt a pair of paws wrap around my leg and a soft little bite on my ankle. Yep, I'd been claimed. We took him to the vet, did all the necessary things, and made him our second indoor feline unit, with the name Smokey. He loves high places—the top of the refrigerator, the top of our kitchen cabinets. We call him Smokey the Mountain Lion.

Our resident housecat, Junior, wasn't happy about this invader, but he soon warmed up to Smokey. Junior had a playmate to keep him active, Smokey had a wise older brother to train him, and they kept one another company for the better part of a decade. When Junior passed away, Smokey was heartbroken. But within two weeks of his brother's passing, we adopted a four-month-old kitten, Gilda. Now it's Smokey's turn to be the wise older brother. He's doing a good job.

Jodie Peeler

Read Gilda's story on page 11.

Read Junior's story on page 19.

Lucy — Before

Lucy — After!

Lucy

In August 2018, we decided to try and find a dog to keep Dodger company.

My daughter had a friend who ran a rescue organization. She brought Lucy over to our house to meet Dodger and to see if they would get along. We immediately fell in love with her. Lucy was five years old and very timid because she had been abused for a long time. But she learned to trust us. She loves to cuddle, and she follows me wherever I go. She's not much on playing with toys, but I don't think she ever had a toy until she came to live with us.

When Lucy goes out in the yard, she hops around like a bunny, and she likes to chase the squirrels. Lucy will sit for at least an hour and just watch the squirrel up in the tree. Dodger and Lucy get along pretty well. She follows him around a lot, too!

We love our Lucy very much, and she is a joy to have.

Margaret Fox

Read Dodger's story on page 15.

Moose and Red

For the past fourteen years, Moose and Red have been canine best friends. Moose is a blue Italian greyhound who came into our lives as a puppy, who lived as an only dog until he was three years old. We thought he needed a friend, so we adopted Red, a red fawn Italian greyhound, who was approximately one to two years old.

Any concern we had about Moose adjusting to his new brother was unfounded. In fact, they bonded from the start. Red's background is unknown, but Moose taught him it was okay to walk on grass and how to use stairs.

Moose shared his house, humans, food, and toys with Red. They did everything together, whether it was attending Italian greyhound playdates or other dog-friendly events. We soon learned that walking them separately was not an option, as Red howled and paced the house until Moose returned.

Now that the boys are seniors, they remain inseparable. No longer social butterflies, they only have each other for canine companionship. Moose now has compromised vision at age sixteen years, while Red has significant hearing loss in his advanced age. They act as each other's eyes and ears. Romps in the yard have been replaced by naps on the couch, huddled together under soft blankets. Sometimes they have squabbles typical of brothers, but their bond remains unbreakable.

I cannot describe how much I love them and how much they mean to me, and I am truly blessed to have had them in my life for so long. When they do leave this world for whatever comes next, I have no doubt they will remain together, best friends always.

Loretta Sisco

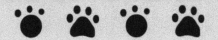

Gidget

Neighbors often laugh at Gidget's antics, whether she is spinning in the direction of every car that passes her on her walk—and if two cars are coming from opposite directions, oh my…what a dilemma for her!— or simply jumping at least halfway up my front door in a greeting to anyone who passes. Gidget loves life from the movement she wakes up until it is time to rest up for the next day.

Though quite the kisser, I'm not allowed past the front door without getting a face full of puppy kisses, which ***does in fact*** brighten any day! Gidget is not the snuggler I had hoped. She does, however, know when her affections are needed. The last weekend of my father's life, when he was quite ill, Gidget ever so gently kept nuzzling his hand, as if to say, "Grampy, it's me, Gidget, I love you," which made my heart ache with sadness and swell with love at the same time.

Gidget is my sweet, little nudge.

I hope everyone gets to experience the love of a pet at least once in their lifetime. It is nothing short of the ***BEST***.

Heidi Perret

Frank

I first met Frank (short for Frankincense N. Purr) nearly sixteen years ago. I had just moved with two cats to Western Massachusetts after living in the Boston area for a long time, and my roommate brought him home from a local shelter. He was so small that he fit in my palm, and his overly large ears comprised most of his heft. The tag on his neck read "Honeyman," the name the shelter had assigned to him, and it was obvious from the start that it was a fitting moniker: he lovingly attached to me immediately and established one of his favorite pastimes to be rubbing his face on my forehead when I would lie on the carpet next to him. To compensate for his petite frame and balance out his sweet disposition, I gave him a name I thought evoked toughness: Frank. I naively believed this would offer him some "street cred" among the alternately growing and shrinking group of other rescued cats with whom I shared a residence.

Frank grew, but not as large as his feline companions, and he often assumed a submissive role in the pet hierarchy, even when he became the elder statesman of the bunch. After I bought a house, friends asked why I didn't expand my menagerie to include a dog, and my answer was always the same: I didn't need a dog—I had Frank. As uncharacteristic of a cat as it seems, every day, Frank met me at the door when I returned home. He always came running to me when I called his name, and nightly, slept on my ankles at the foot of my bed.

When Frank was only seven, he developed an overactive thyroid and had to stay in the hospital for a radioactive iodine treatment. He had been an indoor cat his entire life, and anytime my spouse and I spent time in the backyard, Frank would stand at the window and cry incessantly. In his short stay in the animal hospital, he cried as well—the entire three days, likely driving the staff nearly insane. When my husband returned to the clinic to bring Frank home, he could hear our little man calling from the boarding cells out of sight.

To this day, I don't know if I'll ever have another animal companion who is so loyal and loving. I am very blessed that Fate delivered Frank, my forever honeyman, into my life.

Rebecca Rowland

Maggie

Maggie graced our lives in the Winter of 2009. She spent her early months with our chocolate Labrador mix, Abby, who taught Maggie everything she knows. After Abby passed over the Rainbow Bridge, Maggie's job was mostly to be a companion to Granny, as well as be the resident family love-bug. Maggie is a big, sweet girl with a gentle soul, and her favorite things are breakfast, dinner, treats, walks on the beach, chasing squirrels and bunnies, treats, walks around the neighborhood, more treats, basking in the sunlight (and did I mention treats?). Maggie's least favorite activity is going to the vet and getting her nails clipped, but she knows she has to do it if she wants to run around and have fun. She is always up for being squeezed and adored by family and strangers alike. Her best friends are Jasper, a Border Collie mix, and Harley, a fellow yellow Labrador pup. Maggie's family could not be luckier to have her as a part of it.

Adele Pandolfo and Nicole Pandolfo

For Abby's story, see page 51.

For Harley's story, see page 63.

For Jasper's story, see page 71.

Benny
a.k.a. 'Wild Wheel'

You may ask why I have another name—Wild Wheel. Well, it felt like a decade ago that I was a "race horse." My race name was Wild Wheel, but most people call me Benny now. When I was first looking for a home, I was a difficult little ham. Then I found the most wonderful animal lover—Bridgette—who was determined to find another partner to work with and love. After six long years of love, hard work, and travelling, Bridgette and I are at a new barn where I have another little girl, Rylee, who loves me so dearly. I have a great life with both my girls and my friends in the pasture. I love to jump and can't wait to start showing and competing as the weather gets nicer!

Translated from Neighing-ish to English by:
Rylee Dodge

Annabelle Lee
(The Seer)

"I see dead people," Annabelle may say to you if you understand her "mep mep" speak.

I have a clowder of cats who live with me, and Annabelle considers herself the Queen of the Clowder and seer of all things—including spirits. She came to live with my husband, Peter, and me unexpectedly on the day Peter broke his ankle. She was a rescued kitten and quickly made her way into his Peter's heart. She kept him company and bonded with him through his recovery and into his unexpected death not even two years later. Annabelle immediately started bringing me meaningful and unexplainable signs from Peter after his death. She also picked up on my grief whenever I was feeling sad about Peter and would either cuddle with me or bring me another sign of comfort from Peter. Animals are a great source of healing in emotional times.

Veronica Ochipinti Menard

Tiny

It had been a few years since my dad had declared a "no more pets" policy, yet every December, "A Dog" had been at the top of my list for Santa. Then one Christmas morning, when I was seven or eight years old, I unwrapped a hand-written gift certificate and soon found myself at the shelter picking out my very own puppy!

I remember peering through the glass into a room where a litter of rambunctious little mutts—a Shepherd/Hound mix—were clambering over each other yipping, "Pick me!" All except for one very small one, cowering in a corner. Not surprisingly, it was Dad—Mr. "No More Pets" himself—who pointed out that sweet little runt, and when they let me hold her, I knew she was the one.

On the way home, I was charged with naming the new pup. "Anything you want," they said, "she's your dog!" I rattled off a few suggestions: "Brandy!" (well, no—that sounds like the drink)… "Gypsy?" (nah!). Finally, I took a good look at that little brown head with the big brown eyes just poking out from inside my mom's half-zipped coat, and I said, "Tiny." Well, everyone knew she wouldn't stay that little, but somehow it just fit.

Tiny was a sweetheart. She greeted me every day when I got home from school as if she hadn't seen me in weeks. She kept Mom company when Dad had to work nights, and she listened patiently when my sisters needed a sympathetic ear. She liked to lay with her paws dangling over the third stair from the top, keeping watch over the family. And she loved riding to the Jersey Shore and always got excited at the first whiff of salt air.

That wonderful little Christmas gift stayed with me right through college. We grew up together. We called her Tiny, but she will always be an enormous part of my life.

Jeff Reim

Milly

This is Milly, my three-legged wonder dog. One misjudged leap (and landing) as a puppy led to an open fracture, a steel rod implant, a staph infection, and finally, the decision to amputate her back leg. She handled it all like a champ, and a year later, passed her therapy dog certification exam with Therapy Dogs International.

From the first visit, Milly was a natural! The hospital started sending us primarily to two places: the operating room waiting area (anxious pre-op patients and their families) or to the orthopedic rehab floor, where amputees would take one look at her and fall in love. Milly and I have many stories from her therapy dog visits, but I have one particular favorite. The woman was in a pre-op waiting area. As she hugged Milly, she explained to us that she was an animal lover who had spent many years operating the county's Animal Control office. Her duties included the difficult task of confronting animal abusers in person, intervening to rescue pets from harm. I told her Milly had actually come from Animal Control—in the same county—in 2014. She stopped, looked at Milly, looked at her husband, looked at me. "Is this…? She could be…?" Their memory aligned with what I had been told. Milly, her mangy littermates, and their malnourished mom had been seized from a flea-infested shed in the middle of summer—a backyard breeding situation concerning enough that neighbors called the city. The woman sitting here had been the one who answered the call and drove out to rescue the pups. Now, she and Milly looked each other in the eye with wonder. She promised to look over her records. Weeks later, I received an email with pictures of Milly's litter and a copy of the adoption paperwork with my name on it! She wrote, "To think…I helped her when she had no place to go, and four years later, she sat by my side and comforted me just before I walked into a major surgery. Amazing."

Lydia Phillips

Buddy and Buster

For many years, my Florida home was also home to many fur kids, until a couple of years ago, when I became an empty four-legged nester. I've always wanted a Maine Coon cat, so when a small female Maine Coon became available for adoption, I agreed to a meet and greet at a local pet store, even though I've always been partial to males. This poor cat was not very sociable and scared of her own shadow, but I agreed to adopt and socialize her.

As I was signing the adoption paperwork, I—along with everyone in the pet store—heard a commotion coming in the front door. Two women, each pushing a store cart loaded with everything a spoiled cat would need, along with cat carriers on top containing two screaming cats, approached the adoption table. While removing one of the cat carriers from the cart, the handle broke, and it landed at my feet. All I saw was a black and white cat. The rescue folks asked if I would be interested in adopting these two cats that just arrived instead of the Maine Coon. They were everything I was asking for in a cat—except they weren't Maine Coons. They were Manx—twins born at the cat rescue four years ago. Their heartbroken fur mom had to rehome them because of a serious medical problem that left her unable to care for them. They had all the records for the boys. I was not familiar with Manx cats, so I called a friend, who said, "Yes! Take them!"

Needless to say, Buddy and Buster found a new home. Buster, who is charcoal and white, spent the night behind the washing machine, and Buddy who is gold and white, stayed in the kitchen— close by to Buster. Manx do not have a traditional long tail, but a short stub. I still laugh while watching them wiggle their little butts as they walk or run. It only took a couple of days for them to become acclimated to their new home. They spend most of their day outside in the screened-in patio and pool area, where they have a special bench they use to watch the birds, squirrels, and the occasional rabbit. And they are always on guard for lizards that wander into their domain!

My empty four-legged nest is now a four legged home.

Marilyn J. Slaughter

Abby

Abby has moved on from this world to the next, but during her time on earth, her family was the luckiest family around. She originally came into our lives as a support animal for our emotionally demanding black Labrador, Bernie, but she soon became the favorite pup of the family. She was a very rotund, chocolate lab with a white patch on her chest, and she was truly the gentlest soul on earth. She loved indulging in Italian pignoli cookies and chasing after squirrels, birds, and rabbits in the backyard. Her favorite thing to do was run in the giant field across the street from the house, and get squeezes and cuddles from her family. One of her most unique traits was that she could never really go to sleep if someone was still up—even if it was two o'clock in the morning and she was (dog!)-tired. You could look over at her and see one bloodshot eye opened wide, making sure everyone was safe and okay before she herself could rest. We miss you, Abby, and we'll love you forever!

Nicole Pandolfo

My Milo

"Hägar the Horrible" was the name on the cage when I spotted this curled up creature in the corner of it. I walked around to see his eyes. Yes! They were blue! I was picking out a cat for my cat, Chloe. My mission was to find one that looked just like her to trick my landlord; I'm only permitted one animal in my apartment. The coloring was right, but why was he given this name? I asked to pet him and even to hold him.

"I don't know," they told me. "He's aggressive."

I started to pet him, and I gained permission to pick him up.

"Why is he named that?"

"He was hissing and aggressive while caged" (in a big room with barking dogs, overnight in a shelter, mind you).

"Can I take him home?"

"I'm not sure if he's adoptable."

Well then—why is he here?! I was told he hadn't been eating, and they were concerned for him. I could take him home overnight for a trial period, even though they usually only allow trial periods for dogs. But if he doesn't eat today, then I need to bring him back because he could get sick if he goes much longer without food. I took him home and got him set up in my bathroom. He squeezed into a tiny little space under a cart, into which I never would have imagined he could fit! I placed some dry food in front of him and hesitantly he reached out with his paw, pulled some in closer, and started to eat! Next step: a new name! I was thinking of something regal, but nothing seemed right. I needed to get to know him better. He slowly came out of his shell as he felt safer in his new environment. He was timid, scared even…and *playful*,…doofy,…cuddly…and sweet. That's when I knew! *Milo!*

Now how Milo and Chloe adjusted to each other is another story entirely!

Corrine Ochipinti

Heather

I've always loved animals, and as far back as I can remember, I've always had a pet—from fish, to birds, to cats, and to dogs. When my sister and I were little, my parents got us a Golden Retriever—Heidi. And I loved Heidi. But after years of watching Lassie, my little heart was set on a Collie. And like Lassie, I wanted a Collie with a blaze—the signature white mark on Lassie's nose.

My aunt in New York State, who trained and showed dogs, found Heather, a Collie from a champion line. But Heather was not placing well in the shows, and as a result, her owners decided to sell her to my aunt for me. Her original owers insisted, however, that because of her champion line, we were not allowed to spay her and had to "keep her whole."

While Heather was the family dog, she was also truly *my* dog. She slept on the bed with me at night, and every day, I'd race home from school to see her. We'd go for walks around the block and play in the backyard, which included hide and seek around the woodpile and our above-ground pool. Sometimes she'd go swimming in the pool, too. My dad would lift her and Heidi up and place them in, and they would swim with all of us. *Simpler times.*

Heather lived a happy life with us until the early 1990s, when she developed breast cancer. We knew when it was time for her to leave us, and on the day we put her down, we had a vet appointment at four o'clock in the afternoon (the earliest they could take us). I sat with her all day, right by her side, stroking her beautiful fur, helping her through her last hours until it was time for my parents to take her on her final trip to the vet to cross the Rainbow Bridge.

Heather and Heidi were a tremendous part of my childhood. They will never be forgotten.

Carol M. Ford

Read Heidi's story on page 73.

Bad Boy Bear

I got Bear when he was two months old. Bear is a Teacup Yorkie. He only weighed two pounds when I got him. He was born in Austin, Texas. Bear flew from Austin to Houston, and then to Philadelphia, where I picked him up. He would steal my pens and hide them, as well as play with the keys on my laptop.

Bear is a service dog and works with autistic children. Bear loves people! If you met him and did not pet him, his feelings would get hurt. Bear loves to play with the ball first thing in the morning. He finds one of his balls and throws it so it hits my leg, which means it is playtime! When he has to go out to go to the bathroom, he rings a bell to let me know he needs to go out. Bear also hides his bones all over the house.

Bear doesn't mind being dressed up throughout the summer. He wears his sunglass—and keeps them on! He loves swimming, boating, getting his belly rubbed, and playing. Bear even has a New Jersey driver's license (but he cannot drive a car!).

I am so lucky to have such a great dog and companion. I am so glad Bear came into my life.

Jody Sandberg

Ozzy

If you weren't already a cat lover, you became one after you met Ozzy. He was a super friendly Russian Blue mix who we rarely called by his given name. Like our other animals, he had plenty of nonsense nicknames, including Buzz, Buzzlebutt, and Scuzzlebutt.

He was a curious, green-eyed kitten when we first met, climbing into my lap for attention, confident I would choose him over his littermate to take home. He succeeded, and this loveable little guy had me wrapped around his paw from the beginning.

Ozzy enjoyed the life of a well-loved, healthy housecat until he was three years old, when his medical issues began. Over the next decade, he endured multiple tests and treatments for his various conditions. He tolerated food changes, strict medication regimens, and hospital stays, but through it all, he remained a gentleman and a model patient. He always had a pleasant attitude about his situation, even during the worst bouts of illness. If cats could smile, he would have had a perpetual grin. That's how sweet he was. Although he was chronically ill for eleven of his fourteen years, his issues were well managed, and he lived a good life with few setbacks. I miss him terribly.

Ozzy may have answered (or not, in typical cat fashion) to a variety of nicknames, but the inscription opposite his photo in my gold locket is the most fitting—"The Four-Legged Love of My Life."

Loretta Sisco

Jupiter

My turtle, Jupiter, is a little rude but also very sweet! Here is Jupiter's story.

One summer day, my mother woke me up saying that my dad had a surprise for me out back. I went outside, and I saw this thing that looked like a rock just sitting on our deck. I came closer and found out that it was a box turtle. My dad accidentally hit him with a lawnmower. We were worried that he wasn't going to make it, so we took him inside put him in a big box with water and fruit and headed to the store. When we got home, Jupiter was out of the box!

We kept Jupiter through the winter, and he finally started eating. After a while, I came into the room where he lives, and I saw turtle eggs in the cage! That's when I found out Jupiter isn't a boy! Jupiter is a girl! Did you know that turtles can hold eggs up to seven years? We incubated the eggs, but sadly, the eggs didn't make it.

Jupiter is living a happy life with me!

Isabella Ochipinti

Harley

Harley Rae, a high-energy pup of eight weeks, came into our lives in June 2018. She is our yellow Labrador, and nine months later, she still has no "Off" switch. From the moment she opens her beautiful, green eyes, she plays hard and non-stop, always on the move. When she finally passes out from exhaustion, there's no doubt she will squeeze her 65-pound body into whatever space is available, so she can nestle with her sweet head into the crook of an arm or the bend of a leg.

Harley enjoys playing fetch, long runs on the beach, and rummaging through the trash for leftovers, but her favorite pastime seems to be challenging herself to destroy indestructible toys in record time. Her dislikes include baths, pedicures, the vacuum, and being scolded.

Harley has brought indescribable joy to our home, and we are so lucky to have her.

Michelle Gill

Josie Cat

Some people are hard to get to know; they might be overly quiet or avoid social situations. I've learned that cats can be the same way. Josie Pussycat (who I sometimes called Bob because of her solitary, bobcat-like antics) was found abandoned in a barn, and although she joined my household at only two months of age, she never really shook that feral experience, avoiding any interaction with humans (or other cats) for most of her life. In our first apartment together, I tied a string toy to the middle of a doorframe, and each of my furry roommates—I had four at the time—took turns batting it about. When it was time for Josie to take a try, she immediately grabbed the toy in her mouth and made a run for it. When the string snapped, she happily raced away from her colleagues, proudly chomping on her trophy.

Josie kept to herself for the first decade and a half I shared with her, often sleeping alone while her fellow cats crowded the bed at my feet. But after she turned fifteen, out of the blue, she began creeping into bed next to me, purring in my ear and demanding attention, which I happily welcomed. It became our little routine, her snuggling up next to my shoulder as we drifted off to dreamland in tandem.

Six months later, she stopped coming to bed. She stopped coming out for meals and refused to leave her solitary perch on the futon in a back room of the house. Only a week after that, she passed away, her tiny body riddled with the cancer she had hidden so bravely until it became too much for her to bear. She was independent until the end; Josie was my bobcat warrior and my friend.

Rebecca Rowland

Razzi: The Razzle Dazzle Dog

In late Autumn 2008, we welcomed a noisy, naughty Samoyed named Ms. Raspberry Krinkle into our home. She was Sammy #7 for our family, and we instantly realized something was very different about this girl. She was showy and precise in all her movement; determined in every undertaking; impatient with anything boring, accompanied by her signature 'krinkle' or grumping. Yet still, at times, was this comedic persona you just had to laugh at. A fashionista always, Razzi was tough, intense, and oh...so brilliant. Lessons weren't necessary—just show her.

Our first years together were tumultuous as we tried to bond with this difficult little dog. Kind people called her "unique." The behaviorist called her hypervigilant. We called her "the varmint." She would always be that unpredictable, independent, often arbitrary girl with her own agenda. Life could be an exhausting battle of wills over something silly. Motherhood and daughter Cachet put the Razzle Dazzle in a better place. She was now the canine pack leader and could give her people a break. Still our most difficult dog ever, we fell in love with Mom Razz in the whelping box and never looked back.

In July 2014, devastation in the form of Razzi's lymphoma diagnosis shattered our world. Three to four months with chemo was the prognosis. We were shocked, hopeless, and oh so angry. Panic stricken is how we operated that first month, always afraid it would be the last day. Who knew we'd be together for twenty-two months?! Our journey was as enjoyable as possible thanks to the care and concern shown by Kingston Animal Hospital (Kingston, MA). With Razzi responding amazingly well to treatment, we were a family project. The hospital angel Gina would keep advising, "Enjoy the present, it is a gift, one day at a time." We were able to appreciate the Dazzle for the day and kept making memories.

Razzi also transformed through these months. The reality of lymphoma brought us closer than we had ever been. One most special miracle was Razzi choosing to depend on and trust us. Spending so much time together, the rules and regulations came down, and we so enjoyed being together. We just got comfortable. We came a long way from where we began. We learned life lessons and made awesome memories during this amazing ride. Our family has been changed for the better, forever.

Michelle and Stefanie Harris   67

Señor Juan Lopez

Hola! Me llamo Señor Juan Lopez. Como estas? I am doing very well, thank you, and am *sooo* happy with my new life. My mistress Veronica, a social worker, found me as a little guy, not even two months old, outside the home of one of her patients. I was thrown out of the window of a moving car, and then they tried to run me over! I was lucky when Veronica rescued me and brought me home with her. I had a broken tail and a bruised voice box, but Veronica takes really good care of me.

I rarely talk, but my purr is like a motor. As soon as I think someone is coming over to give me attention, the motor starts in anticipation. I also love to ride around on anyone's shoulder who will let me do so and can lift me! I am now eighteen pounds and have been nicknamed "El Gordo." I am also quite talented—I'm self-taught in turning pull chain lights off and on, flushing the toilet, and drowning toy mice, so I don't leave an unnecessary mess for my mistress.

I want Veronica to know how much I appreciate her choosing me and giving me such a loving home.

Translated from Meowish to English by:
Veronica Ochipinti Menard

Jasper

Jasper is a Border Collie mix that came into our lives as a rescue pup named "Patrick's Brother." He was born in Tennessee, and while we're not quite sure what happened to Jasper and his brother Patrick in Tennessee, we do know they were rescued after being left in the woods and surviving a vicious coyote attack. Jasper made his way to a rescue organization in Boston, and then eventually moved with his family to New Jersey. Jasper loves to play fetch with a ball, hike, and sleep in the middle of the bed. He is always up for herding everything, from small children to dogs, to vacuums, and even cars, if he is tired enough! He is incredibly intelligent and often outsmarts his humans to get extra treats and ball throwing. His favorite way to pass the time is chewing an antler bone next to his humans on the couch who love him more than anything!

Nicole Pandolfo and Dan Gerlane

Heidi

It was 1977, and I was eight years old. We had just moved into our new home in Southern New Jersey, and I was missing my friends back in our old neighborhood in Pennsylvania. My parents decided that to help my sister—who was five—and me adjust to life in a new place, they would get us a dog.

My aunt—also an animal lover who trained and showed dogs, had a stable of horses, and owned a menagerie of cats and dogs—was up to the challenge! She found a Golden Retriever puppy, and Heidi soon found her way to her new home with us.

Heidi (nicknamed "Bubbie" or "The Bubs") was every bit of Golden Retriever as one could imagine. Playful to the max, her favorite toys were her Woobie, a stuffed rag of a thing, and her Nubbie, a toy pacifier. She loved to eat! And she loved people—all people! Everyone who came to visit was coming to visit Heidi, don't you know? When my Heather, my Collie, joined the family, she was the perfect "big sister" to Heather. She roughhoused with all of us, and you could do anything to her. Pull her tail. Tug her ears. Yank on her rough. She didn't have a mean ounce of anything in her body and was all love.

Heidi developed several "fatty" tumors over the years, as is typical for Goldens. But one tumor was not a fatty tumor, but sadly, was a brain tumor. She ended up going partially blind and deaf, and after almost fifteen years with us, she crossed the Rainbow Bridge. To this day, my mom will still get teary when she thinks of Heidi, who was truly her dog. Heidi, who stayed by my mom's side at all times, even protecting my mom when a swarm of bees attacked her. She went after those bees and snapped at them buzzing around in the air, trying to keep my mom safe.

Play and bark and run, Bubbie. We'll see you again one day.

Carol M. Ford

For Heather's story, see page 55.

Stanley, the Hangar Cat

Meet Stanley. Stanley is a large, tiger-striped tomcat who resides at the Liberty Aviation Museum in Port Clinton, Ohio. Stanley's story is a good one. It seems he started life out as a pet, with people who fed and cared for him. But the people moved away and abandoned Stanley. He was forced to fend for himself, living under porches, getting food wherever he could find it. One of our museum employees, Eric, took pity on Stanley and started leaving him food outside. After a period of time, Stanley gained enough trust in Eric and came to live with him. Once again, Stanley had a home. Shortly after that, due to circumstances beyond his control, Eric was forced to give up his place, and for a short time, lived in the visiting crew quarters in the museum's big hangar, bringing Stanley with him.

After being an outdoor cat and fending for himself, Stanley was very wary of people. He would not let anyone pet him anywhere but the top of his head. If you tried touching his back or sides, he would become defensive, using his teeth and claws. But as time went by, Stanley got used to all the different people who work and go through the museum, and now he interacts with them freely. In fact, he often follows tour groups as they make their way through our display hangar, becoming the center of attention.

There are several areas in the hangar that Stanley is not allowed to be in, such as the gallery room or the lobby. We learned just how smart he is when he taught himself how to put the doorstops down, so when the door is opened it doesn't close all the way, giving him access to the forbidden areas. Stanley has truly captured our hearts with his sweet personality and zany antics. He seems to be very happy here and is well taken care of. So if you are ever in the Lake Erie Islands area, stop by the Liberty Aviation Museum and say hello to Stanley, the hangar cat!

Terence Murray

Shemp

This is my newest member of my household—Shemp. I got him right before the New Year. He was a Christmas present to myself. Some of you may be familiar with my other cats from the first edition of *Golden Linings*—Moe, Larry, and Curly.

Back on August 28, 2018, Curly crossed the Rainbow Bridge. He had been having really bad health issues to the point of losing over half of his body weight. He just wasn't doing well anymore, but he is now pain-free. Many of my friends and family would ask me, when will I get a Shemp? As with some pet owners, I wanted time to grieve and was in no rush in getting a new cat. I briefly checked out one in the fall, but it just wasn't the right time.

Fast-forward to Christmas 2018. My sister-in-law told me about a cat she saw on Facebook who was at the Voorhees Animal Orphanage. When I saw the photo of a cat named Cephalo, I was intrigued and drawn to his chubby face and big head. Of course, I wondered why he was given that name and discovered it was very appropriate. It is a direct reference to the size of his head! But Shemp *had* to be his name.

When it comes to *The Three Stooges*, Curly was always the first love for fans, but some don't realize that Shemp started as a Stooge with Ted Healy. He didn't last long and was quickly replaced with Curly. Here's the interesting part. During Curly's career, he suffered a stroke. So he couldn't act anymore, and the movie studio brought in Shemp. Curly eventually succumbed to a heart attack, and Shemp became the newest Stooge in the slapstick trio.

So I find it very strange that my Curly died, and eventually, my Shemp came into the picture. All I can say is he is a 13-pound lovebug that loves to snuggle and be petted. If I stop petting him, he will nibble at my hand to let me know not to stop. It took some time before Shemp and the other two knuckleheads would get along. But all is well now!

Darin Peters

Bama

In July 2013, we were visiting family in Gulf Shores, Alabama. In between beach time, my husband Calvin, daughters Julianna and Jessica, and Aunt Danielle drove to the phone store to fix my daughter's phone. As they got out of their car, they noticed a lady setting up a table and a hand-written sign that read "Free Puppies" on the side of busy Route 59. She was giving away six of them—the entire litter! Curious drivers began gathering quickly when my littlest, Julianna, picked up the fluffiest white one with a brown face. Another lady took it from her arms with disregard! Jessica picked another fluffy white one with light brown spots, and he was to become our keeper. Aunt Danielle chose a puppy, too—a fluffy, white one but with a few black spots.

Picking a name for this guy was fun with everyone's input. Scuttles was an option; there was also Nutella, Cocoa, and Snowball. Ultimately, we decided to name him Bama after his state's namesake. Aunt Danielle named her puppy Jersey to memorialize where she grew up and the place where Bama would soon make his forever home with us. We were told the puppies were a Chi-Weenie-Pom mix and wouldn't get to be more than ten pounds. Bama is a whopping thirty-four pounds! We think perhaps our pup is part Jack Russell Terrier. Do you see it too?

Bama joined our golden retriever Duke back at home, and it took just a few days for Duke to warm up to him. Bama really didn't give him a choice; he jumped on, tugged, nuzzled, and chased Duke until he would give in. They quickly became best buddies. Bama is a quick learner. Watching Duke obey commands, he picked up a few commands himself! Duke crossed the Rainbow Bridge in 2015, and we have since brought Bama a new playmate, a rescue Pom-Chi mix who really is as small as they said she would be, at twelve pounds. Pebbles and Bama, a match made for *The Flintstones*…I mean, the Watsons.

Jennifer Watson

Empty Collar

My Letter to Sherman's Breeder

You may not remember me, but several years ago, I purchased from you two Australian pups who I named Sherman and Molly. They were littermates.

It is with an extremely heavy heart that I write to you to say that Sherman passed away on Thursday evening. He hadn't been himself for a while; most days normal, some days not. He couldn't keep weight on. That day, after I came home from work, I knew. But I was hoping he would bounce back the next day like every other time.

I had a gig, and I asked my mom to stop by around 7:00 to check on him. She said it was around 8:00 when it happened. He wasn't alone, thankfully. She was petting him and talking to him the whole time. But I wish I was the one there.

My belief is that it was cancer. He had an extremely healthy appetite, to the point where I switched over to diet food a few years ago because he and Molly were getting heavy. His "moods" were not always consistent these last couple of months. As I mentioned, most of the time he was Sherman being Sherman. Other times, he could barely move, but he'd usually return to himself the following day.

I decided against getting an autopsy done because I was told that he'd have to go to the University of Penn, and it would cost anywhere between $500-$800, and they might not even be able to give me the answers that I needed. Plus, ultimately, those answers weren't going to bring him back to me.

continued on page 81

Sherman, Molly, and Ernie (my Corgi) were always connected to my hip. Everyone always commented on how amazing they are/were whenever they were around people. I never got around to taking them to obedience training or agility training. Sherman never learned any tricks or commands beyond "sit" or "kennel time," when it was time for them to go into their crates. On the leash, walking all three was like holding back a tornado. But off the leash, they were amazing, always responding when I called them back to me, even when a cat, a bunny, or another dog appeared.

Sherman absolutely was a kissy face, with an endless supply of kisses for people, especially me. His demeanor was sweet, playful, people-friendly, dog-friendly, boundless energy level. He was a lap dog. He was so in tuned with my mood; if I was upset or angry about something, he would pick up on it and stay clear, especially if Mr. Angry Voice came out, and he would get upset. But if I was laughing about something on TV, he was all over me, kissing my face. He couldn't get enough attention. Although Ernie liked to play, if Sherman saw me getting involved, he would eventually demand that I remember that he was the belle of the ball.

He and his sister Molly were definitely brother and sister. They cared for each other, taking turns licking his/her eyes and face. Although middle-aged, he and Molly would still battle it out like they did when they were puppies in my kitchen, with Molly eventually giving it to him to show who was boss. Sherman instantly became Ernie's big brother when I got him. Always patient when this little puppy was jumping all over him and biting at the fur around Sherman's neck and face. He *never* got upset. And up until Thursday, Sherman and Ernie could be found in the back yard chasing and playing with each other.

continued on page 82

I could write for hours and hours, and still have things to say about my Baby Boy. To say that I'm devastated would be an understatement. It's cliché to say, but he really was my best friend. Although I love Molly and Ernie, the house just isn't the same. It was always the three of them. It was always the FOUR of US. We were a pack.

I just wanted to let you know, and to THANK YOU for allowing me to have the most amazing dog ever. I think that you mentioned to me that there was another family who originally wanted him, and they brought him back for some reason that I can't remember. All that I can say is that they missed out. I still remember being at your house, after deciding that I wanted both of the "twins" (Sherman and Molly), and just

was watching them. There was a couple there who I could tell wanted one of them. So I raced out to an ATM and took out the money so that I could buy them right then and there. Looking back, I would have paid ten times that amount for what I got in return. I'm sorry that I didn't get to bring them around more for a visit. Life just got in the way.

Again, thank you.

Daniel O'Neill

CAROL M. FORD has worked in the publishing industry since 1997. She earned her BA degree with Honors in English/Liberal Arts from Glassboro State College (now Rowan University) in Glassboro, New Jersey. She is the Director of Editorial Services, an editor, and a managing editor for Anthony J. Jannetti, Inc., a health care association management, marketing, and publishing firm located in Southern New Jersey near Philadelphia. Working with nurse leaders, she oversees the production of several clinical peer-reviewed nursing journals, publications, and textbooks. Carol is the author of *Bob Crane: The Definitive Biography*, which details the life of the late radio personality and *Hogan's Heroes* star, and among other written works, is the editor and owner of *Golden Linings*, a charitable book series that raises money for shelter and rescue animals. She is owner and CEO of Carol M Ford Productions, LLC, established in December 2018. In addition to managing podcast post-production services for clients, she is also currently producing a new podcast about Bob Crane called *Flipside: The True Story of Bob Crane*. Carol resides in Southern New Jersey with her two fur-kids: Copper, a golden retriever, and Charley, a rescue cat. Visit Carol's website at www.carolmford.com to learn more about all of her work.